The Road Home

J.John

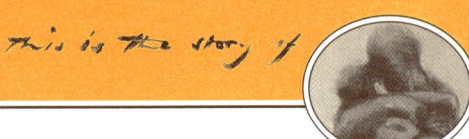
This is the story of the prodigal son.

Copyright © J.John 2005, 2025
First published by Philo Trust in 2025
www.jjohn.com

The right of J.John to be identified as the author of this
work has been asserted by him in accordance with the
Copyright, Designs and Patents Act 1988.

All rights reserved. No part of this publication may be reproduced or
transmitted in any form or by any means, electronic or
mechanical, including photocopy, recording or any
information storage and retrieval system, without
permission in writing from the publisher.

ISBN: 978-1-912326-35-8

Print Management by Verité CM Ltd
www.veritecm.com

Printed in the UK

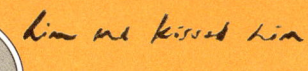

DEDICATION

I dedicate this book to Charlie Mackesy
(who painted the cover) who creatively communicates
the Father heart of God without words.

this is the story of  the prodigal son.

Personae

Francis Nutrizio — Steward and narrator

Theodore Salvadori — Master of the Salvadori Estate

Katerina Salvadori — His wife

Andreas Salvadori — Their elder son

Yiannis Salvadori — The younger

Despina Aristophanes — Lady-in-waiting

This is the story of the prodigal son.

ran to him and hugged  *him and kissed him*

CHAPTER ONE

Five short, blunt words. Beating at the door, ringing in my ears, shouting at the window on a dark, clear night; driving me to God-knows-where, to a place I might have glimpsed but not yet seen; bereft of grid reference or signpost.

Which way do we go?

The future is an empty horizon. The past slips away like the wake of a boat sailing to the edge of the known world. Soon I will be gone. Yet in the turmoil of a world turned upside down, a still, sacred moment of presence offers itself as a lifeline. In the eye of the hurricane, it can suddenly seem eerily still. And in this deepest of nights, in the stillness of a moment held captive, one simple question demands an answer before time is released once more and day breaks like a wave on the rest of my days.

Which way do we go…?

My name is Francis Nutrizio. And for most of my life

This is the story of the prodigal son.

I have kept a meticulous record of my master's business. But now it is time to tell of my own. And I have just one night to do so: huddled at this old, familiar friend of a table, wrapped against the cold in a blanket and searching for words by the light of a single flame. Although it is late, sleep can wait like a dog outside the door. For who cares if I am tired tomorrow? After twenty years, it is my last day as steward to the Salvadori family of High Florent.

First, I must explain how I came to be in this position as steward to the House of Salvadori, serving the good Lord Theodore and his two sons. My own family are not of this region; the House of Nutrizio is noble enough in the west of our country, and I will never know what made my grandparents move far to the east. But whatever it was, it was not a wise move. The result was a life of poverty, for both themselves and their children. My parents, despite their terrible fortune, retained their dignity and were fiercely ambitious – if not for themselves, then at least for me. From the earliest age, they drove it into me: work hard

ran to him and hugged  *him and kissed him*

and make a good name for the family and myself. Reputation mattered. *Our* reputation mattered.

When I was barely thirteen, hell came calling. It was a winter's night and a candle was left carelessly alight as we slept. My father had probably drunk a dram too much spirit to warm his soul. But warm him it did. I thought I was dreaming of the lake of fire until I awoke to blood red flames raging through our house. Miraculously someone, somehow saved me (to this day I know not who); my parents never even made it out of their room.

An aunt took care of me. She was kind, if not adoring. She did ensure that my education continued and four years later, aged seventeen, life took a turn – the kind that you hardly notice at the time but on looking back, you can see quite clearly that it was a fork in the road. And this was my turning point: I had the good fortune to join the Salvadori family in the upper part of the Florent Valley.

This is the story of 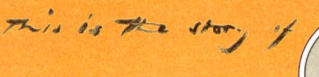 the prodigal son.

As the estate is remote, the family is renowned for recruiting orphans who do not need to spend days away visiting their families. Upon my arrival as a fresh-faced young man eager to impress, I set to work: first, as a junior clerk in the steward's office – the kingdom of the unforgettable Marco. Marco was a thick-set man whose eyebrows joined at the centre and who, whatever the weather, dressed like a raven in thick black robes. He always laughed from the depth of his belly, especially after three or so jars of his favourite dark ale with the locals from the town; yet for all his merriment, he was widely feared; Marco knew everything and everyone, and he knew exactly how to get what he wanted from them.

My apprenticeship with Marco, however, was the opportunity of a lifetime and only a fool would not have seized it with both hands. I worked harder than a donkey, finding out how every aspect of the estate worked. My father, and later my aunt, taught me never to accept bribes – for this was dishonourable –

ran to him and hugged  *him and kissed him*

and soon my reputation spread as a trustworthy man. Over the next two years I learned my business inside out – the jobs that needed to be done, and how, so that the estate would run smoothly and efficiently. I soon knew which tenant farmers we could trust to pay us on time and which would need one of Marco's dreaded 'visits'. And I learned the challenges of each different season: to repair the cisterns before the rains of winter; to hire men before the ploughing season; to stock up with wood before the snows made the high forest inaccessible to our horses and mules.

Marco began to entrust me with more and more. And why not? It made life easier for him. Soon, I was supervising the shepherds' accounts – a difficult task, because they are unreliable and untrustworthy (and who knows how many sheep a shepherd really has?). But I succeeded in my task, and within another eighteen months I was running the tenant farmers' accounts. And, by my twentieth birthday, I was accompanying Marco to meet with the Lord Theodore

This is the story of the prodigal son.

himself. It was an incredible privilege but a daunting task. The first time I entered his rooms, I was concentrating so hard that I almost tripped and fell headlong into a chambermaid. Gradually, I found that I need not worry. My Lord Theodore was a kind man and sympathetic to my nervous stuttering (although he only asked who I was, and how I was, and whether I had learned to count properly at school, unlike the tax collectors…). In time I found that the rumours were true: Theodore and his wife, the Lady Katerina, disliked Marco but had come to find him indispensable. I also learned another lesson: that the good steward has little to fear – only the most foolish of masters gets rid of a competent steward.

Just after my twenty-first birthday, Marco grew ill and I found myself taking on more responsibility. No one quite knew what was ailing him but on a cold spring day when the winds blew across the mountain and rattled at the shutters, Marco winced with pain, clutched at his heart and toppled from his chair.

ran to him and hugged  *him and kissed him*

He lay on the floor, a great, charcoal mound that heaved, and then fell still. The raven was gone without so much as a goodbye. I was immediately appointed acting steward, and in the following weeks my Lord looked for a replacement but no one more suitable could be found. Of course, there were those who said it was wrong and too big a risk to leave someone so young to manage the accounts. Still the Lord Theodore, who had little time for honour or shame, overruled the objections. So there it was: at the age of twenty-two I became steward at this beautiful estate.

Although I did not know it, in the twenty years since I joined, I would witness the household at its greatest time. Our estate was one of the largest in the Prince's realm. It was like a great, wide spoon of land that straddled the River Florent as it flowed down from the mountains of the north to the great rocky gorge in the south. While much of it was flat meadowland by the river, it also ran up either side to the high foothills of the mountains. If you were to ride the borders of the

This is the story of the prodigal son.

estate – and I often did just that, especially in summer at sunset, when the light made the river shine like liquid gold – it would take three days. In the upper reaches, we would have to dismount and walk through the dark woods and mountain pastures. Sheep grazed the pastures, and the woods yielded timber for building and firewood to keep us warm in winter. On the descent, you passed through terraced slopes rich with fruit orchards, olive trees and vineyards. Towards the Florent, the land gently eased into meadows for cows, fields full of wheat and ponds for fish. A number of springs bubbled to the surface there, few of which failed even in the driest years. The land was kind to us.

In fact, we had everything we needed. My Lord Theodore once turned to me and, with a smile of contentment, declared, 'Francis, this is not just an estate; it is a world.' And he was right. Had pestilence or war sealed us off, we could have lived well enough on what we had in the valley alone. As it was, we traded profitably with the towns and cities below us.

ran to him and hugged him and kissed him

The house lay at the heart of the estate. It stood proudly on a mound; a broad, graceful building supported by columns and crowned with a terracotta roof. I have seen other great houses and many of them were adorned with towers, battlements and high walls. But the great House of Salvadori was different; it was, as someone said (using the old Latin word) a villa. It was surrounded not by high ramparts but by low walls, by gardens and hedges. It was open in both appearance and spirit. It boasted a lofty timbered hall with balconies and a great fireplace which kept it warm in winter when the winds blew off the icy mountaintops. A stone's throw away, and separated by a pencil line of poplars, stood the offices, stables, workshops and servants quarters. And scattered around the house and the offices were nearly two hundred cottages – for those who depended on the estate.

But an estate is not just the land and its crops; it is the family. I began to serve the Salvadori household when the Lord Theodore was in his forties; he was tall and

This is the story of  *the prodigal son.*

well built and moved with impressively youthful energy. I came to know and love him well and, as I write, I grieve his passing, which is fresh. Theodore was an intelligent, thoughtful and compassionate man. I might have added 'pious' but Theodore had little time for the religious leaders of the town and their banal rituals and was, by all accounts, considered by them to be irreligious or worse. Yet in private he was a man of faith and reverence, a thoughtful reader of the Holy Scriptures. He cared for his people and they, on the whole, cared for him. He gave them work, enforced laws, built schools and provided a doctor, and was the willing and generous sponsor of celebrations and festivals.

Theodore ruled the estate with wisdom and grace. Yet he was a reluctant leader; he had been the younger of two sons and it was only his brother's tragic death from a hunting fall that made him heir. When, in due course, his father died, he was obliged to take on the estate out of a sense of duty. At times, he must have

wished he could escape from this role and the burdens of management. Once, as we drank a glass of wine together after another long day, he confided in me that as a youth he wanted to leave the valley and travel to see the wide world beyond. As he spoke, he stared out at the road south and I caught a wistful yearning in his face.

Perhaps his reluctance to take the job explained his occasional insensitivity to the demands of honour and decency. He was a man who was irritated by the constraints that tradition and duty place on us all. This disrespect for tradition was clear even in simple things, such as the way he carried himself. Everyone knows how a ruler of any sort, even the master of a large estate, should move: slowly, solemnly with decorum and dignity and always without haste; he should never perspire and never look flushed, urgent or hasty. To do so is to lose dignity or, as we say here, to lose face. But Theodore did not seem to care; he never possessed what the ancients called *gravitas* and cared little for the manner and style of power and position.

This is the story of  *the prodigal son.*

Here is as good a place as any to record my only complaint of him: that his generosity of spirit would often undermine my own position and authority. I valued kindness as much as anyone but as the head of an estate, resolve and unwavering firmness is vital. Each autumn I would work through a list of our tenant farmers, draft their bills and dispatch them. But within days I would inevitably find myself summoned to meet Theodore in his study, which was piled high with books and furnished only with two simple chairs and a battered table. There, standing on the threadbare carpet, I would see another teary peasant clutching their bill. Inevitably, Theodore would tell me how his heart had been touched by the unprecedented plight of this particular farmer and how – if I concurred – he would like the sum to be reduced or payment postponed. Of course, I had no option but to bow my head and acknowledge his wisdom and generosity. He did not do it too frequently (and no one ever got away with it more than once or twice) but still, it undermined my

...n to him and hugged  *him and kissed him*

authority. The wise ruler runs his estate well by strengthening, not weakening, his steward's authority.

Of the Lady Katerina, I have fewer memories, for she died over ten years ago. But I cherish those memories I do have, of a small woman who was merry and carefree. When I visited the house I would often hear her singing. Strangely, Theodore treated her as an equal partner, something unheard of in our land, almost shocking and, many believe, dishonourable. After all, in our world it is deemed right that while women are to be treated with honour and praise, they are also to keep silent and it is best for them to stick to their own concerns. But Theodore would have none of that. Sometimes he would invite me into the main room where the Lady Katerina would witness our deliberations, quietly sewing or making some tapestry – but listening to every word. Often, Theodore would pause in his conversation with me and turn to ask for her opinion. It was, I thought, quite odd but this *equality* that he granted her also hinted at what was to come in his relationship with his two sons. But I jump ahead of myself.

This is the story of the prodigal son.

My master and the estate remained at the centre of things. Every month, the lords of the adjacent lands – the Mouzakis from the west, the Tavionos from the east, the Carreris from the south – and sometimes others – would ride up with their carriages and finest horses to visit. My Lord would hold court in the villa. It was a fine gathering of nobles and the honour that they paid to my master was gratifying: he was held up as their head and his advice was sought and taken. The lords would gather around a long table and after wine and mezes, there would be much discussion of important matters.

I felt privileged to be there, seated behind my master. Frequently in the discussions he would tilt his head back towards me, I would lean forward and he would whisper to me questions such as 'How much does the House of Tavionos owe us?' or 'How much are we getting for figs and olives these days?' and I would whisper back the answer. He would nod and, armed with the facts, turn back to the discussion.

I watched closely at these meetings and listened with the greatest care, preparing myself for those moments when my master would need my knowledge. Seated there, slightly in the shadows, I could keep a close eye on things. My Lord Theodore was certainly respected – people rose when he entered, kissed his hand and smiled at his humour. He came from a distinguished line and our estate was the most prestigious around. But this respect was tinged with a darker edge; behind the bows and careful words, I noted carefully how they all watched him. There were those who would like to have bought land from him; others hankered after more generous contracts with our estate and some were deeply envious of his position.

Once a year in May, my Lord Theodore and I would ride to the city, where he and I would meet with the Prince's managers to discuss and agree the tribute due to the Prince. On the following day, my Lord would meet privately with him and renew his oath of loyalty. And then we would return. The sight of our carriage gliding

This is the story of the prodigal son.

over the crest of the hill and down the long drag to the town would be the signal for joy and celebrations.

They were golden days and it is not just the benefit of hindsight that tells me so. There were threats of war, rebellions and famine, but they all passed by our valley. It was by no means a perfect world but it was as happy as they come in these imperfect times.

Chapter Two

*N*ow you know the background, my tale must proceed quickly. The first rays of dawn will soon be scoring the darkness, when I must away.

Within a year of my arrival, Lady Katerina became pregnant and the first son was born on a warm, late spring evening when the storks were flapping northwards overhead. They called him Andreas. We spin our children the familiar yarn that storks bring babies and with Andreas it was easy to believe. Three years later, a second son was born in midsummer and he was named Yiannis. Theodore's happiness seemed to be complete. He had two sons and the future of his family appeared to be secure.

Yiannis was one year old when I was made steward and I came, of course, to know him and his brother well. It is easy, looking back, to trace the seeds sown of what was later to come; the boys were always so different from each other. However far back I stretch for my

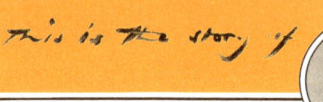

This is the story of the prodigal son.

recollections of Andreas, I always remember him as a solemn, thoughtful and watching child. Yiannis was different: lighter in complexion and manner, a carefree, relaxed boy who wanted to explore everything. It was easy to like 'Yianni' as he came to be called by many. I refused to use this shorter name myself; it would not have been proper. It was a mark of the difference between the two that Andreas similarly would not allow any abbreviation of his name.

As they grew up, both boys would visit my office. Andreas would stand alongside me, look at the accounts and ask what I was doing. Sometimes I would let him play with the bright counters and he would sit and make columns with them before returning them in neat piles. Yiannis would also come but if it were the counters that attracted his attention, he would help himself and scatter them in a mess upon the floor. When he grew bored and wandered away, I would have to retrieve them – on my hands and knees – from the four corners of the office.

to him and hugged  *him and kissed him*

Yiannis, however, soon acquired an interest in reading books, and from an early age was often to be found in the library reading fiction, tales of far distant places and of traditions other than our own. As he grew, he would leave the house and wander through the town. Of course my master was so highly respected that he never came to harm and sooner or later a workman would carry him back on his mule or over their shoulder, to be rewarded with a few shiny coins from Theodore. Occasionally, Yiannis would climb the watchtower by the stable and gaze out into the distance, down the dusty road that ran up the grey hills and out of the valley.

Although Yiannis's free spirit made him an attractive child, from a very early age he showed signs of disrespect. He would saunter into my office, even when I was busy in negotiations, and tug at my coat, demanding, yes *demanding* that I give him some counters or some paper to write on. Of course, as he was my master's son, I granted his requests but it was

This is the story of the prodigal son.

not proper. I could see the amusement written on the faces of those I was trying to deal with and felt shamed. I could recall many similar instances. There were some who said that his father should have disciplined Yiannis earlier and more severely. But it is not the task of a steward to judge how his master runs his family.

The two boys never really got on with each other. They were, by temperament, like chalk and cheese. I found I liked Yiannis but did not respect him and whilst I respected Andreas, I couldn't warm to him.

As the boys grew, so did my role. Theodore came to put the highest trust in me. I rode with him everywhere and he and I came to be as close as a steward and master could be. In fact, he seemed like a father. The weather was kind to us in those years; the crops flourished, the estate prospered and all was well. In my fifth year as steward, the Prince himself visited us and stayed for three days. I had never faced a greater challenge; my work was unrelenting but all went well

and the Prince left us greatly pleased and lavished my master with praise.

And on the great days, the feasts, the Saints' Days, when the flags would fly and the drums and trumpets sounded, I could not help loving this estate and being proud of all that we had come to be.

I had been given the house that Marco had previously filled with his brooding presence. It was too big for me but I made it comfortable. I lived prudently. Sometimes I considered marriage but I had found no one suitable; I held to the maxim that a steward's position, midway between his lord and his people, is delicate and he must therefore choose his wife carefully. Sadly, in such a small town, there were few families with whom an alliance would have been appropriate, and those that there were had no eligible daughters. I wondered about finding a girl from the city but I was there so rarely that I knew few people and besides – who would have let their daughter go and live with me? So I made the best of my situation and reconciled

This is the story of the prodigal son.

myself to a life of domestic solitude, which I eased by reading books from my Lord's considerable library. In fact, as I threw myself increasingly into my work, my periods of leisure were few.

As I have said before, when you are wandering down the road of life it can sometimes take a subtle, yet significant turn. And so, in my tenth year at the estate, my Lady Katerina acquired a lady-in-waiting, Despina Aristophanes. Despina was from the city and also an orphan but unlike me from no family of name. I had never heard of the Aristophanes and neither, it seemed, had anyone else. In fact, I thought she was common and lacked the dignity that servants in such an intimate role ought to have. She seemed a rather strange creature, with long dark hair, a thin face and sharp brown eyes that had a way of looking at everything with an amusement that seemed most improper.

At first, I had little to do with Despina; the only interest a steward has in his Lady's maidservants is

their cost to the estate. Increasingly though, she made her presence felt – and we soon clashed. She had the audacity, having only just arrived and hardly having had time to unpack her things, to come to me with a list of items that she wanted for her room. I stared at her with incredulity, and asked to see the Lady Katerina's signature of approval. She replied with a brazen look that it was what she personally wanted. I explained, as calmly as I could, that this was not how things worked around here. She glared back. 'Steward Francis,' she said, in a voice loud enough for others to hear. 'That may be the way that things worked in the past, but I would like another way. My lady has granted me authority to make such requests for myself.'

This display of arrogance, from someone ten years my junior and newly arrived to the estate, was maddening. But I bit my tongue and bowed, explaining that I would have to seek clarification and thus postpone any decision. When I consulted with my Lord, he blushed and admitted that his wife had

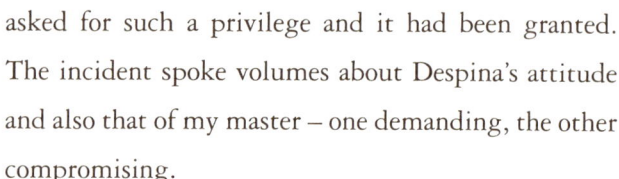

This is the story of the prodigal son.

asked for such a privilege and it had been granted. The incident spoke volumes about Despina's attitude and also that of my master – one demanding, the other compromising.

A year after Despina had swept into the household, the Lady Katerina fell pregnant again. How I wish that the storks really did deliver our babies! Childbirth is a dangerous business and thus it was proved, most grievously. We had prepared to throw one of our famous celebrations yet instead we turned to darkness and mourning. There were 'complications' – a euphemism if ever I heard it, for goodness knows what it was that killed her – and, just like my mother and father, and Marco, our Lady Katerina disappeared from the road of my life without warning. The baby, a girl, died later that day. Perhaps it was just as well. A shadow fell across the whole estate.

Had my Lady Katerina lived, events in the future might have been different.

...n to him and hugged  *him and kissed him*

Chapter Three

My Lord grieved passionately for his wife. He refused to shave for weeks, and life seemed to drain from his face. He might have been present in body but his spirit was surely elsewhere, searching for his lost companion, shouting from the hills, chasing through the valleys where she loved to walk, but never catching up with her. For months I found myself making decisions on the estate. Then slowly, wearily, reluctantly, Theodore hauled himself back from wherever he had been; dawn began to rise on this long, dark night of the soul, and slowly he began to reassert control. After all, we needed him. And deep down, he needed us.

When the Lady Katerina left us, I expected Despina to go too. She had other plans, however, and stayed firmly put. She took charge of the female workers in the house and in so doing, undertook a lesser, domestic counterpart to my job. We now met more frequently and I admit that, slowly, I acquired a

This is the story of 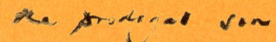 the prodigal son.

sneaking respect for her. Anyway, a steward must learn to put his own feelings to one side and I could see that she had competence and honesty. And I saw that she, like me, seemed to find her purpose in service to the Salvadori Estate.

Respect is not affection, however, and she still displayed that infuriating disregard for matters of honour which I cannot abide. Her dress and way of speaking were never formal for a figure of her position, and she should have taken more care with whom she associated. Once, as I rode past the market, I saw her down in the stalls shopping and she was laughing and joking with the merchants. She saw me and didn't even have the humility to look chastened. I think this was partly her upbringing, but I felt that it was something that Theodore had encouraged by his reluctance to impose his will on her in such matters. They were, it would seem, kindred spirits.

For the purpose of my tale, I can skip through those years. It became clear to anyone who had eyes to see

ran to him and hugged  *him and kissed him*

that trouble would arise with the children. On the face of it, Andreas was the model son: hard-working, diligent, aware of his destiny, forever riding around the estate and watching the proceedings with a stern eye. He took to giving orders to the people and although at first this seemed amusing, as he grew up it became irritating and presumptuous. It undercut both my authority and that of his father and eventually we issued a ruling that while Master Andreas was to be honoured, all orders were to come only through myself or from the Lord Theodore.

Yiannis, however, gave the greatest cause for concern with his many escapades. On one occasion, for instance, while in his early teens, he wandered into the drinking house during a night of peasant dancing and I had to rescue him from under a table where, after too much to drink, he had fallen asleep. Another time, he vanished overnight and we later discovered that he had spent the night under the stars, as if he was a tramp. In each case, Theodore frowned and had angry

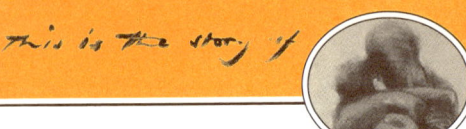

This is the story of the prodigal son.

words to say – but nothing more. And in each case, after a brief respite, the tension would surface again.

By the time I reached my twenty-first year with the estate, Yiannis was eighteen and, from what I could see, craved freedom. He argued regularly with his father, though I did not pay the fall-outs too much attention as they did not involve me. However, one April evening while I was working late in my office, the door opened and in walked my Lord Theodore. I rose to my feet and bowed; he closed the door behind him, took a seat and sighed. It was not unusual for my Lord to consult with me, but normally he asked for me to come to him. It is the way such things are done.

'May I talk with you?' he asked, quietly.

'Of course, my Lord' I replied, surprised at his tone and concerned by the troubled look on his face.

He hesitated, leaned forward towards my desk and started fiddling with some pencils. 'I have a difficult problem to resolve,' he said in a slow, strained tone.

'I would like your advice.'

He looked up at me with sad eyes.

'Of course, sir,' I replied. 'I understand that you are often given difficult questions to resolve.'

'Quite so. It is a delicate case. A younger son wants to take his inheritance in a sizeable estate and leave.'

I stared at him, but he seemed to avoid my gaze.

'My Lord, that is unusual but not a real problem. After the death of the father, an estate is divided and it is our tradition that the elder has two-thirds, the younger has a third. Normally both would keep their property. But, in theory, the younger could do as he wished. I do not see a problem.' I was rather tired and wondered why he had bothered me with such a straightforward case.

'There is a problem. The father is not yet dead.'

'You mean...' I paused, trying to get my mind around the appalling case. 'The son – the younger son – wishes

to sell what would be his before his father dies?' I was aware of the tone of incredulity in my voice.

He nodded.

'That would be extraordinary. No, *unforgivable*!' Theodore raised an eyebrow, and I continued, 'To ask for an inheritance before a father dies would be an insult of the highest order. It is equivalent to saying to one's father, "I wish you were dead". The family in which it happened would be subject to the deepest shame.'

Theodore's face paled and a bell of warning sounded in my mind. Surely not, I thought in sudden alarm; he cannot possibly be referring to Yiannis.

'Nevertheless,' Theodore said, in a weary, dogged way, 'suppose that the younger son wished it. Should the father allow it?'

I could see, now, that Theodore was not adjudicating for others. He was agonising over the situation with his own son. I felt my jaw drop and saw him catch my expression. He flushed with shame.

ran to him and hugged  him and kissed him

I didn't know what to say. It was all I could do not to stutter. 'My honoured and respected Lord, the wisdom of our lands and of our traditions is that such a request should be refused. Indeed, sir, it is such a dishonourable and shameful request that I have to – reluctantly – say that tradition demands that the child be beaten for even making it.' I stumbled on. 'Sir, such a request undermines the way we live. It shows disrespect to the family system. It breaks with honour and honour, as you know, is the cement that holds together the building of our society. To allow for such a decision would be to encourage other similar acts.'

He said nothing but kept fiddling with those awful pencils. The implications were flooding in now, all of them serious. 'My Lord, for a man to allow such an insult to be unpunished would be to approve of it. It would be badly viewed both by his subjects and his neighbours for similar reasons.' I caught my breath. 'Furthermore, this is not simply a case of blind tradition. Were this landowner to fall ill, it is the duty

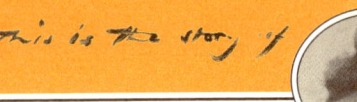

This is the story of the prodigal son.

of his sons to look after him. And if the inheritance has been squandered, how can he be cared for? Were it to happen such a man might find that in his old age he was reduced to begging.'

'Indeed.' The single word was all he said.

Silence descended, but it was so awkward that I had to fill it. 'And to sell ancestral lands is neither right nor honourable. We and the land are linked…'

'So,' he spoke, looking at me, into me, through me, with his stone grey eyes: 'You would not advise that such a request be granted?'

Self-preservation began to take over. 'Sir, I am a steward. The job of a steward is to advise on the wise running of an estate. I could not, in all honesty, support such a decision.'

He sighed. 'Francis, I value you enormously and I value your honesty and wisdom. You know, of course, that the one I speak of is Yiannis.'

ran to him and hugged  him and kissed him

I will not forget the moment as long as I live.

'My Lord, I had wished that it was not so.'

He cleared his throat. 'Were the request to be granted…could it be done?'

'It would damage the estate. A third?' I shook my head. 'The best you could do would be to surrender to him the eastern high pastures; the Sefarians would gladly buy that patch.'

Without a word, he rose and went to the open window. He breathed in and stared east towards the pastures that glowed red with the setting sun.

'Sir,' I asked, 'what would he do with the money?'

'I do not know, Francis. He talks about travelling. He is a restless young man. I sympathise with him. I was once like him.'

I hesitated but felt I had to say more. 'Sir, you have shared your confidence with me and I ask in turn the right to speak freely. I would urge you please to consider any decision gravely. It would damage your

This is the story of the prodigal son.

estate, your future and your reputation. It cannot even be said, with certainty, that it would be for the good of the young man.'

My words were audacious; for a steward to tell a master how to treat his son is to cross a well-marked boundary. But thankfully this was no ordinary master. 'Francis, you are right. But life and love mean taking risks. And to let him go will hurt me enormously.'

He walked to the door.

'But thank you for your honest advice. It is a father's dilemma.' He sighed. 'If only Katerina were here to advise me.' And with that, he was gone.

I wasted no time in arranging a secret meeting with Despina. Faced with a crisis of such magnitude, it was time to ignore any reservations about the way she handled things. She had heard the rumour and, to her credit, was also perturbed.

'Miss Despina, surely it cannot be allowed? The implications for the estate are appalling. His name would suffer shame.'

ran to him and hugged  him and kissed him

She stared at me with searching, brown eyes – I had never noticed how brown before – and she shook her head. 'Sometimes, Francis, I wonder whether you understand him.'

'How do you mean?'

She clasped her hands together, held them up to her face and stared thoughtfully at me over them. 'Francis, you live for honour, for the name of a thing. He sees that it is the thing itself that matters.'

I felt myself frown.

'He is faced,' she continued, 'with a terrible choice. Either to let Yiannis go free or to keep him in the valley. If he does the one, he puts his son in a cage. If he does the other, then his son may yet learn to fly.'

I found it hard to read her expression.

'But Miss Despina, if he lets his son go, he will lose him.'

'And Mister Francis…' she replied, teasing me for the formality of my titles. 'If he tries to keep him, he will

most certainly lose him.' For a woman who was not a mother, she was disarmingly wise.

'But the estate will suffer.'

She smiled. 'At least we are no longer talking about honour now. Yes, it will suffer and your job is to do what you can to minimise such losses.'

'I see.'

She gave me a mischievous look. 'Yes. If it comes to making a settlement, don't let Yiannis know the details. Don't give him all the money and keep some back in a hidden reserve.'

'Why?'

She was rising from her seat. 'Because, much as I love him, Yiannis is a young fool and I think he'll make a mess of it. And what he doesn't know he has, he can't spend. There may come a time when he will need the money.'

'I see,' I muttered, but she had already left.

ran to him and hugged  him and kissed him

CHAPTER FOUR

As we feared, the deal went ahead. It took a month to arrange and the Sefarians agreed, as I expected, to take the eastern high pastures and half the slopes at a reasonable price in gold. A clerk from the city drew up the documents, overcharging us as always. The money was transferred and much but not all of it was placed into an account for Yiannis at the city bank. Yiannis had such little business sense that he didn't even bother to check whether it was all that was due to him.

A few days later, Hendrik, the ex-soldier who manages the watch and the patrol of our boundaries, told me that the Sefarians had been moving flocks into the pastures. The man lacks subtlety of any kind, and clearly didn't approve as he muttered and spluttered his words of criticism, shaking his head bitterly with resignation. Although I would not voice it, I felt the same.

This is the story of the prodigal son.

These things, though, were the easier parts of the affair. It was the gossip in town, the widening of eyes, the shaking of heads and the wagging of tongues that was simply unbearable. We were collectively dishonoured. Not only that but with the transfer of the land, more than ten families lost their livelihoods; they, of course, were furious. And those upholders of our values and standards, the judges and priests, frowned upon the sorry situation and our behaviour.

A week after the deal had been signed, I was tidying my paperwork in the office when there was a furtive knock on my door. It was Yiannis.

I bowed to show him the respect I did not feel.

'I've come to say thank you,' he offered.

'It is my job. My duty is the welfare of the estate.'

'I know you do not approve and I have not come here for your blessing,' he said.

I hesitated before responding. 'Master Yiannis, this will not go down as the greatest event in history of the Salvadori family.'

ran to him and hugged  *him and kissed him*

Yiannis lifted his head and stared me straight in the eye. He betrayed a look of indignation and pride that I had never seen in his face before. I felt uneasy but matched his stare. He walked briskly over to my desk, clutched a sheaf of papers and waved them aggressively in my face. 'You live for these things, Francis. I don't.' His voice was hard and passionate. 'I want more than this. I want to be free! To live outside this compound and the rock walls of this valley.'

I froze, as a wave of anger rose within me. What was this talk of freedom? How dare he belittle the world that his family lived and breathed! And what of our dear Lord Theodore? Hadn't this young man's carefree nature become a selfish lack of regard for anything but his own indulgence? I steadied myself and drew a deep breath. 'Do you care nothing for your home?' I started with a tone more of sadness now than anger. 'What of your father? Do you not love him, Yiannis?'

'I have my own life to live, Francis. I'm leaving tomorrow at dawn.' He spoke his words in a cold,

this is the story of the prodigal son.

formal voice. I sighed and raised my hand to shake his but he ignored it. With a stiff nod of his head, he left the room.

The next morning, even before the sun rose, Yiannis slipped away and quiet descended. It was not an easy, proper quiet however. That he had been allowed to take his inheritance – that he had not been properly disciplined – would have many lasting consequences. Many people were angry with him for being an ungrateful son, of course; but they were livid with Theodore for daring to allow it. And the aftershock of this earthquake was felt way beyond its epicentre in the valley. The neighbours did not meet together that month. They all made their excuses: one family had ill health, another had business issues to deal with, still another had an engagement at the Prince's court. Worst of all, in late May, when we journeyed to the city to pay our taxes, Theodore was not granted his usual interview with the Prince. The message was plain: Theodore had undermined everything they stood for and should be punished.

ran to him and hugged him and kissed him

Andreas said little but he had never been talkative. Instead, he scowled. Once, I caught him once leaning against the wall of the villa looking towards the eastern heights that no longer belonged to his family, with a face that was purest poison. Although he was glad to see the back of his brother, he plainly disapproved of the decision to sell the land. I rarely saw him talking to his father and, when I did, there was a great deal of strain between them. He was hardened and became increasingly withdrawn, but I still had to respect his ongoing dutiful work for the estate.

And Theodore himself? I'm afraid he made matters worse. There is a time-approved way to treat children who have rebelled. It is harsh but logical; you behave as if they were dead. If he had done so then things might have been easier, but he didn't. In fact, he did the opposite. He made little secret of his longing for Yiannis to return.

Two months after his son had gone, he summoned me to the villa for a meal. We ate together on the balcony

This is the story of  the prodigal son.

and talked of the estate, but neither Yiannis nor his departure was mentioned. Finally, as the sun dropped over the hills, the bats wheeled above us and the music drifted up from the village, he came to the reason for my visit.

'I was hoping you would do a favour for me.'

'I serve you, my master. Whatever you wish…'

'I would like you – quietly – to go down to the city and ask about the whereabouts of a certain young man.'

Inwardly, I groaned; I had hoped that the dreadful matter was buried.

'My Lord, I am willing to do this – but is it wise? What if the Prince gets word? It would bring yet more dishonour to your house.'

'Francis,' his voice became stern. 'I have had enough of the word honour. I love both my sons and I want Yiannis back. Go to the city and search for him. Go to the port if you don't find him. I have a small portrait you can take. Make copies there.'

And so I had no choice. Faithful steward that I was, I packed and set off for the capital, ostensibly to see the Prince's managers but carrying in my saddle-bag the portrait of Yiannis and a bag of gold. Once there, I disguised myself as best as I could and set about making discreet enquiries. In truth, I hoped I would find the son and persuade him to return. It would be messy but if he were punished – perhaps made to work on the fields for five years – there might be an end to the whole unhappy episode. But it was not to be.

Instead matters were worse than I had feared. The story of how my Lord Theodore had let his son go free – disregarding all the rules of honour – was talked of widely in terms of a scandal. I was informed that a news sheet carried an article on the subject, and sermons were being preached in church on the need to punish rebellious sons. I heard these tales, shook my head at them and admitted that the world was in a sorry state for such things to happen.

Finally, after much careful investigation, I learned of a rumour that Yiannis had made for the coast. I rode

This is the story of the prodigal son.

there – a hard day's journey – and found that he had, indeed, taken a ship across the sea to a distant land in the south. I gave a copy of the portrait to Captain Shakira who regularly sailed that route and who seemed as trustworthy as any seafarer. I left him my address and asked that when he next passed through that port, he make enquiries about Yiannis. A pocketful of gold was the price for his absolute discretion.

I took my time riding back to our valley. The only consolation was that Yiannis was now making a fool of himself in a land so far away that he could drag our name no further into the dirt. Once I was home, Theodore summoned me with unseemly haste. After all my efforts to disguise the nature of my mission, his action seemed so unsubtle that even the dullest servant boy would have guessed what was going on. I conveyed the news I had gathered, and he walked to the window and stared southwards as if, somehow, he could see across the thousand miles or so to where his son was.

'Thank you, Francis,' he said in a low voice. 'Tell me immediately if you hear of anything further.' It seemed that whenever I visited him through that long summer, he would be standing at the same window, his eyes peering through the heat haze to the shimmering, dusty road below.

I quizzed Despina about how widely she thought news had spread that Theodore was pining for news of his son.

'Everybody knows,' she said, bluntly.

'What happens if he returns?'

'You tell me!' she replied.

'If he's made a fortune, if he comes back in a big gold carriage and throws a big party, he may just get away with it. Success is the only thing that trumps honour.'

'There are other things, Francis…but otherwise?'

'It will be a mess.' She nodded and I continued, 'If Theodore handles it properly, we may survive – if he refuses to see him for three days and sentences

This is the story of  *the prodigal son.*

him to five years hard labour in the fields, then honour may be satisfied. Justice can sometimes remove shame. But he has brought dishonour in every way on the family estate. He has put people out of work. Set a terrible example.'

She gave me one of those looks which made me think she could read my mind. 'Francis, do you really think Theodore will do that? Exact justice?'

'No. But if I hear that Yiannis is on his way back, I will do what I can to make him. The alternatives are far worse.'

She shook her head. 'We'll see.'

For months, no news arrived. And then, as the first snow flurries of autumn had dusted the cloud-wrapped mountain peaks, I received word from the captain. It was a letter which I smuggled to the privacy of my study before opening it. I knew that its contents could change our lives forever.

ran to him and hugged  *him and kissed him*

Dear Steward Francis,

Your friend has made a mess of some business deals. I found him and established that he is the one you seek. He has fallen on hard times. Apparently he earned quite a reputation for himself, throwing his money after wine and women of all sorts. Sons were warned not to trust his word and respectable fathers forbade their daughters to see him. He lived a wild life and has squandered everything. Now he is reduced to taking casual labour of a most unpleasant kind just in order to live; collecting rubbish, working in abattoirs, sleeping rough. I gave him a couple of gold pieces and promised to look out for him again. Knowing that you would reimburse me, I have offered him free passage back any time. But he is a proud soul, even in such dreadful circumstances. Be assured that I am keeping this most confidential.

In your service

Shakira.

This is the story of the prodigal son.

I headed straight to Despina, who let out a deep groan and agreed that it was best that the news be kept from Theodore.

That winter was viciously cold and I found myself glad that at least Yiannis was spared it. As the boats would not sail in winter, I knew that the chances of him returning soon were few. And, sure enough, there was no further news for months. Slowly, the thaw came and spring began to speckle the newly green meadows with fresh flowers. Yet the change in season brought no diminution in Theodore's yearning for his son. Inevitably the person who noticed this more than anyone was Andreas. Once, while looking over the accounts with me, he could contain his bitterness no longer.

'That selfish brother of mine has done enormous damage to our finances. Look at those figures. And still my father longs for his return!' He shook his head angrily. 'The old fool. He should move on!' He spat the words out as if he'd tasted rotten meat. For my part, I maintained a diplomatic silence and continued totalling the figures.

In hindsight, I should have expected the return of Yiannis and I should have talked to Theodore about it beforehand. But hindsight is just that; at the time the matter seemed so difficult that I always managed to put it off. Besides, logic suggested that Yiannis, should he return, would head to the city from where he would send us a humble message asking for reconciliation.

This is the story of  the prodigal son.

ran to him and hugged  *him and kissed him*

CHAPTER FIVE

It was late April, nearly a year to the day after Yiannis had left, when it happened. I was dictating figures to a clerk when I heard feet pounding the flagstones to my door. The door flung open and there was a shout.

'Mr Francis, he's back!'

'*Who's* b–?' I started before working it out for myself.

I jumped up and paced to the door; I wanted to run, but stewards never run. A stable hand had brought me the news and as I strode past him into the courtyard, there was a great commotion. People were everywhere, mouths agape, whispering and staring, pointing down the road.

My gaze followed their fingers and fell upon the most appalling and dreadful thing I had ever seen. Charging down the steps from the villa and out through the gate, his coat flapping behind him and his feet flying wide in the most undignified of ways,

 This is the story of the prodigal son.

was my master. He was *running*. I could have died of shame and embarrassment.

'My Lord!' I cried, but it came out as a squeak as the words choked in my mouth. An under-cook standing next to me began to giggle and I cuffed him, as my turmoil of emotions erupted into anger

'Get me a horse. *Quick!*' I ordered a gawping groom. 'Get Hendrik,' I yelled, 'and the watch.' I turned to the stable hand who had followed me out. 'You are sure it's Yiannis?' I still hoped it was a mistake. But he nodded and I saw that he was trying to suppress a grin. I knew the answer to my next question before I even uttered it. 'Is he wealthy? Has he come with a carriage? On a horse?'

He shook his head. 'He is barefoot. In rags. He has all that he stands up in. No more.'

They brought me a horse which I mounted with as much dignity as I could muster before clattering down after my master, desperately wondering how we could

ran to him and hugged  *him and kissed him*

salvage something, *anything* of the family reputation.

It was too late. Everyone had taken to the streets of the town. Where had they all come from? The press of bodies was so great that my horse stuttered and halted. I tried to maintain dignity as I was jostled by the crowd which was swiftly becoming a mob. Ahead I could see my master, still running, the crowd parting in front of him and closing behind him. Then, as he rounded the corner, he came face to face with the skeletal figure of Yiannis, walking with a stick, the ugly, taunting crowd gathering fast and menacingly behind him.

The sight of him took my breath away. No question now that his adventure had been a dismal failure. I shoved through the people urgently, wishing that I had brought a sword. This crowd was angry. I recognised a couple of men who had worked the fields that had been sold; their faces were burning with rage and they clasped stones in their hands.

I was about twenty feet away from Theodore when Yiannis saw his father approaching. For a moment, it

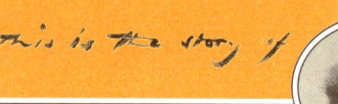

This is the story of the prodigal son.

felt as though the world had stopped turning. Everything was suspended. Then Yiannis opened his mouth to speak but could find no words to bring forth. Theodore stumbled towards his son and flung his hands wide, gathering Yiannis into his arms.

I edged nearer. A gruff voice broke the silence, 'Be careful, Mr Nutrizio. Mobs can be funny. You wouldn't want to be caught up in the middle of this one.' I glanced back to see, with relief, Hendrik and some of his biggest men right behind him.

Theodore must have heard Hendrik. Tears running down his ruddy face, his body heaving with exertion and emotion, he turned to us and gasped, 'He is *back!* My son is back!'

Yiannis lifted his sorry head slowly as his eyes met with his father's. As he spoke his voice cracked with emotion. 'Father, I am sorry. I have done wrong to you. I wish to be treated as less than a servant.'

Yet these words were smothered by the fresh embrace

from his father. Then, in a flash, my Lord Theodore lifted his head, looked around at the crowd and raised his shaking voice. 'My friends – *everybody*, the matter is closed.'

The looks of astonishment were writ large on the faces of the crowd. Theodore turned to us. 'A horse for Yiannis, Mister Hendrik. Steward Francis, please return to the house. Have my official robe and my best shoes ready for my son. Have a bath prepared. Summon the doctor.'

I bowed, as much to conceal my confusion as anything else. 'As you wish, my Lord.'

Then he turned to the gawping bystanders and opened his arms wide.

'My son has come home. Tonight, we will have a celebration at the house. Everyone is welcome.' He turned to me, laughter and joy lighting his face. 'Steward, make preparations.'

'*Everyone?*' I coughed.

'Anyone who wants to come.'

This is the story of the prodigal son.

How could this be? Where within my Lord Theodore's heart could he find such an ungrudging and spontaneous forgiveness? How could he lavish his love so unsparingly upon this worthless and ungrateful son of his? I knew what I had to do. I stood up in my saddle and waved my hat high. I shouted as loud as I could. 'Three cheers for the Lord Theodore and his son, Master Yiannis. Hip, hip…'

An appalling silence seemed to stretch out forever. But then, the response came: a great and growing round of hoorays and handclapping stretched through the crowd, and hats were thrown high into the air. I saw two or three stones drop harmlessly to the ground.

As Hendrik and his men dismounted their horses and led them through the crowd, I turned and rode back. Better to play along with this, I thought, stunned by what I had seen. I had served my master for twenty-two years and I wasn't going to betray him now. Besides, whatever my feelings, I needed to back the old man

now. A steward must manage any crisis that comes his way. If I kept my composure and handled this well, the name of the House of Salvadori might yet endure.

I rode in through the gate, hurling orders right, left and centre. 'Lunis, unfurl the banners. *All* the banners – every one you can find. Karl, heat the bath water. Matthaeus, summon the doctor. Ah Phila, get my Lord's best robe ready – the purple one – and some shoes. Do it!'

I drew breath. 'You, get me the cook. Musa, get every employee who isn't dying, here in their best clothes within the hour.' And looking around, I shouted: 'Everyone! Master Yiannis is back and the Lord Theodore has been pleased to pardon and restore him. It is a day of rejoicing. If I see anyone who isn't smiling they are in trouble. I am less forgiving.'

And there, the face I was looking for. 'Despina, a word please.' I dismounted and we bundled into my office.

'Is it true?' she asked.

'He is back and alive, but barely more.'

'Thank God,' she said, and bowed her head.

'There will be time for that,' I snapped. 'You and I have our greatest challenge.'

'I heard. Theodore has restored him?'

'Totally, publicly. Welcomed him back, announced his restoration.'

She shook her head, and I was sure I could detect the faintest of smiles. 'Extraordinary!'

'I can think of other words for it.'

'You would.'

'My view, Miss Despina, is that he has lost his mind, but that our best hope of salvaging anything from this is to back him.'

She started to say something, but I didn't give her the chance. 'He wants a full-scale banquet with every extravagance lavished upon this feast. Can you do what you can to make it a success?' She closed her eyes and nodded.

ran to him and hugged him and kissed him

'Make sure your ladies sing his praises. Three cheers, that sort of thing. Whatever their private opinions, they are not to show anything other than joy. On pain of dismissal.'

'Very well. There is much to be arranged.' She walked to the door and stopped, her hand resting on the handle.

'Nicely managed Francis. But can I ask you one question?'

'I have barely time but, yes.'

'Do you care that Yiannis has been found?'

I looked at her blankly and confused. 'No, not really. He was a young fool. He nearly destroyed everything we have worked for. He may do so yet. It might have been better if he drowned at sea.'

'There is a lot you need to learn,' she replied, looking hurt.

'I'm just doing my business, lady. You do yours.'

This is the story of  *the prodigal son.*

She slammed the door behind her and moments later the head cook appeared, his fat face covered in shaving foam and his eyes popping wide open. And so we made our plans and preparations.

ran to him and hugged  him and kissed him

Chapter Six

Somehow we got everything arranged. And by dint of threats, promises and nothing short of bribery on my part, we worked wonders. There was enough meat, wine and bread for the whole town. That, in itself, was enough to put a smile on the faces of those who'd been ready to lynch Yiannis hours earlier. But there was also something strangely uplifting about Theodore's disarming act of reconciliation; it seemed to breed forgiveness in others, too.

People wore their best clothes and all was set for a night to remember. I tried not to think of the cost; we would have to meet it from somewhere. We had no choice. As night fell, the front of the villa was bathed in the light of a vast bonfire as the sound of drumming, piping, singing, dancing and laughter rose to the heavens. It was a strangely wonderful sight.

There was just one problem. Andreas was absent and as the evening wore on, I became more and more

This is the story of the prodigal son.

worried. Despina was, too. She'd been scanning the party, in vain, for the eldest son. 'Where is he?' she asked me, anxiously.

'He was up in the mountains checking out the woods for deer hunting. Or so they say. But he should have been back by now. Long before, in fact. The whole region must know we are celebrating something.'

'So why isn't he here?'

'You know why. Because he wants to make a point.'

Sparks flew up from the bonfire and I could see my Lord Theodore, his arm round his second son, strolling, greeting people and being greeted.

'By the way, I'm sorry if I was rude this morning,' she said, under her breath. 'I do admire the way you run things.'

On this strangest of days, I was beginning to see many things in a different light, Despina included. 'No, I am sorry,' I replied. 'I gave you the wrong answer.

ran to him and hugged  him and kissed him

I've been a steward for too long. It has corrupted the way I see the world. I judge everything in terms of its effect on the estate, not in human terms at all.'

'That is dangerous,' she replied.

I was about to agree – I couldn't have agreed more, in fact – when one of Hendrik's men came over and tugged at my elbow. 'Master Andreas is waiting outside,' he said in a coarse whisper that smelled of roasted chicken.

'Thank you,' I replied. 'Excuse me, Despina.' And as I jostled through the crowd, I realised I had addressed 'Miss' Despina the colleague as a friend for the first time. It felt strangely good, like the party itself.

Andreas could have no truck with the air of forgiveness, however. Standing alone outside, his fury and contempt for the proceedings was written across his face for all to see. I bowed. 'Master Andreas, we have been awaiting you. Please, your presence is an honour,' I said as I motioned to the door in more hope than realistic expectation.

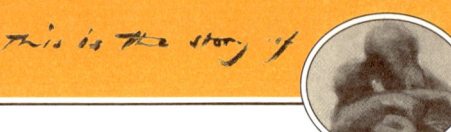

This is the story of the prodigal son.

'I'll be damned if I'll come in,' he stormed. 'My brother is back and my father treats him as if he was a prince.'

'Sir,' I said, pushing my luck. 'It would be good if you would come in.' Something about today was helping me to live dangerously for a change.

'Out of my way, Francis!' he raged, and bundled me aside. There he stood in the open doorway, burning with anger and jealousy, facing the party head on. Who knows if he'd been planning this scene? I have to admit, though, that it was an impressive stand all the same. He was a great oak of a man and the doorway framed him like a picture of strength. I stood behind him, my bravado draining away like a spilled glass of wine. The morning's events were bad enough but this threatened to be worse.

'*Stop this nonsense*!' Andreas shouted, cutting straight through the din of the festivities. Within a second, every drum, pipe and voice had fallen silent.

ran to him and hugged  him and kissed him

He bellowed again. 'My brother is a fool, who has brought shame on us all. He should be punished. He wasted my money, our money, *your* money on *whores.*' The crowd took a sharp intake of breath. 'He took our honour and trampled it in the dirt. Now my father wishes to restore him.' He hurled the words angrily into the room.

And there, from out of nowhere, was Theodore – standing before his son, the same loving look in his eye that had extended to Yiannis. 'Andreas, my dear son,' he said gently. 'You must understand. You brother was lost. I had given him up for dead. He is now alive. Celebration is the only thing that is right.'

For one terrible moment, I thought Andreas would strike his father and I moved closer to intervene, but he lowered his face until it was just inches away from his father's and snarled at him. 'Right? *Right?*! *This* is not *right*! You've never treated me like this. Yet this drifter son of yours gets a *party.*'

'My dear son, *he* was lost.'

this is the story of the prodigal son.

'I have worked for you and for this estate every day for years. I have always obeyed your orders and you have never, ever given me this attention.' A sole tear threatened to betray just how much this was hurting him, as he choked out his words.

'My son', Theodore spoke with such kindness. 'You must give up this lie that I love you less. I love you. I would search for you as I searched for your brother. Everything I have is yours. Do not be deaf to my voice calling you now, to join us and eat.'

But Andreas would have none of it. He turned on his heels and slammed the great door shut. Theodore stood rooted, calm, as all eyes turned towards him. I nodded to the minstrels. Music flowed into the vacuum left by Andreas and slowly, and unsteadily, the celebrations began again.

I placed guards around the villa that night in case Andreas tried something foolish but in the morning word reached me that he had left for the city.

ran to him and hugged 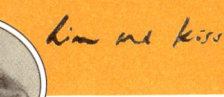 *him and kissed him*

I arranged to meet Despina in the grounds of the villa under the apple trees, which were now thick with blossom. Amid the turmoil, she and she alone seemed to make sense of things. She saw the world from a different angle. And she helped me to open my eyes.

'How terrible,' I said to her. 'He gets one son back and loses the other.'

She gave me that strange, knowing look and shook her head. 'No. He had lost both of them. Now he has found one and the other realises that he is lost.'

I thought about it and realised she was right. 'Despina, will he get Andreas back?'

She smiled, sadly, looking down. 'I am flattered and honoured that you think I can answer such a question. But, of course, I cannot.'

Over the next few days and weeks we slowly settled down. Gossip was rife, of course, about Yiannis's return and Andreas's departure, and the Prince sent an emissary to find out what happened for himself.

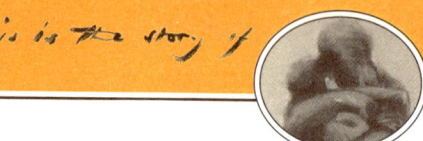

This is the story of the prodigal son.

I didn't see him because Theodore spoke with him alone, telling him that it was family business and that – with all respect – it did not really have any relevance to the Prince. Then he sent him back on his way.

Yiannis began to recover from the rigours of his year away. He put on some weight and started to look like his old self again; yet his manner was much changed. He was now a quieter and more reflective man. One day I was walking through the villa gardens after meeting with Theodore, and I came across him sitting on a seat. He gestured to me urgently to come and sit next to him. I joined him, feeling awkward because I was sure that he knew how I felt about things.

He turned to me. 'Francis, I want to thank you.'

I was genuinely taken aback. 'Whatever for?'

'You handled my return very well. I realise, now, that it could have gone disastrously.'

'Yes, it nearly did.' I said, thoughtfully. 'Crowds are a funny thing. But you need to thank your father.'

'I have. But you helped a lot. You have both showed me such grace. I am so unworthy and yet you and my father have treated me with such respect.'

'Thank you.' I felt ashamed as I knew that I hadn't respected him. 'But my job is to do the best that I can for the estate and for your father.'

He raised an eyebrow. 'I know your feelings. But that doesn't matter to me. You were right and I was wrong. I was a fool.'

A servant is not used to receiving apologies from their master, and I didn't know what to say. So I mumbled something along the lines that I quite understood, and I was sorry if my attitude had been wrong, and I was glad that he had been reconciled with his father.

'What are your plans now?' I asked.

'I was expecting to join the servants, to pay off something of my debts. But my father refuses to allow it.'

'He is a truly remarkable man,' I noted.

'Indeed. I'm thinking of leaving,' he said. 'But with

This is the story of the prodigal son.

my father's blessing this time. I think I can earn a living in the city teaching. All those books I used to read! Maybe Andreas will come back if I'm out of the way. My father would like that.'

I looked at him. He was clearly a changed man. 'Master Yiannis, you may like to know that I – er, I made an error in giving you your money last year. After you had gone, I found that there was a sizeable amount left. It is in an account for you…should you require it.'

He smiled with grateful eyes. 'What a very convenient oversight. Thank you. It may well come in useful.'

A week later, helped by the money I had saved for him, Yiannis moved to the city where he started teaching. Over the next few months, I was pleased to hear that it was going well. Of course, there was never any question of him paying off his debts – he would have to teach for a hundred years to do that – but it was a start. I was pleased to hear that he kept in touch with his father through regular correspondence.

ran to him and hugged  *him and kissed him*

A few days after Yiannis departed, Andreas returned and set himself up in the far end of the villa, as far away as possible from his father. I do not know whether they even spoke to each other. I certainly never saw them together after that dreadful encounter at the party. From the little revealed by Despina, she found herself employed very much as an intermediary.

As summer drifted once more into autumn, and autumn chilled to winter, this uneasy situation continued. And in the first weeks of the new year, it became apparent that Theodore was not well. The strains of the previous months had surely taken their toll, as had the constant, malevolent presence of Andreas around the estate.

In the second month of the year, Theodore descended into violent fits of coughing. We summoned a specialist doctor from the city and Yiannis made his way rapidly back to seek his father, being careful to keep out of the way of his brother. As I paid the doctor the usual extortionate rate for such a professional,

This is the story of the prodigal son.

I asked him privately for his verdict. He looked around to make sure no one else was listening, and shook his head. 'He is coughing blood,' he whispered. 'You should make sure that his affairs are in order. His care now belongs more with the priests than with doctors.'

A few days hence, I was summoned to Theodore's room. There I found a thin, pale-faced man who seemed to have aged ten years in the last month. His doctor sat at the back of the room, keeping watch.

Theodore motioned me over to his bedside. His face may have changed but those penetrating eyes had not lost their look of love. 'Francis,' he said in a low, slurred voice. 'I want to thank you for your faithfulness to me. I have not been the easiest of masters to serve. I know you have, on occasions, disagreed with me – but you've always been faithful to my house, and I wish you well.'

I bowed my head; to receive such praise from your master is the greatest thing that any steward can hope for. I had done my job.

'Do you know, Francis, why I acted how I did?'

'No, sir.'

He put a blood-stained cloth to his lips and coughed violently. 'I could only try to act in the way that God acts.' He caught my look of puzzlement.

'You don't understand, do you? Despina does. You must talk to her.'

He coughed again, painfully, and took a sip of water from a glass.

'God gives us freedom even though it breaks his heart, Francis.' Theodore was not a religious man yet to hear him talk of God like this began to make sense.

I nodded, slowly.

'You think I made myself look like a fool by taking back my son in such a way, don't you?' We had not spoken of those events until now.

'That is not a word I would ever use of you, sir. Now, or ever.'

This is the story of the prodigal son.

Theodore managed a smile. 'Diplomatic to the end, Francis. But I was a fool. I lost honour, I lowered myself – *running* – good grief.' He shook his head slowly. 'I can barely believe it myself. But it was my way of saving Yiannis.'

I nodded again.

'You see, I love him, as I do both of my sons; I love them so much. No price was too high to bring Yiannis back, not even our reputation.' There was that word again. Reputation. He looked at me, smiling. 'When you have a child, Francis, you will understand. Whatever those men do cannot change the fact that they are my sons, and my love for them does not depend on their actions. It will not change.'

I was silent. My Lord continued.

'And you saw the mob, Francis. What would have happened if I had delayed? If I had walked steadily, as is deemed fit and proper?'

'I think, sir, they would have driven him out. Thrown

ran to him and hugged  *him we kissed him*

stones. They were angry at what had happened – at the way he'd acted. And some of them had lost their land.'

'Yes, the mob would have given him justice all right. As they saw fit.' He closed his eyes in pain. 'God preserve us from such justice, Francis. The justice we deserve. Where would any of us be if God used justice alone as a measure?'

I paused. My life seemed to flash before me and I felt the truth of what he said. 'Indeed, sir,' was all I could muster.

'I saved him, Francis. At a cost.'

'Yes, you saved your son, sir. He's a different man now.'

'I'm glad. Do not the priests teach – although I fear they have forgotten it themselves – that God became a man and was mocked? And worse, he was stripped and nailed to a cross, so that he might save his sons from their own mess?'

'They do, sir. But I have never understood it.'

This is the story of the prodigal son.

He looked gently at me. 'My prayer is that you will. God chose to be humbled because he loves you. Me? I was merely mocked as a fool. And perhaps that is all I am.' He seemed to struggle but turned to look at me again. 'You have to take the first step back, Francis. You have to decide to return.' His eyes bore a great sadness but also hope; his voice, now, was almost a whisper. 'The distance is the same for us all, whether it's from a wild rebellion obvious for all to see or just a cold, simmering resentment and self-pity, trapped in the quietness of a heart.'

He coughed again and the doctor came forward from the end of the room to order me out. Theodore closed his eyes and motioned me back. 'But if you return, he will meet you along the way.' A faint smile broke. He was already leaving for another place – in his heart he was probably running again, this time along the road that his beloved Katerina had taken so many years before. I closed my eyes and, for a moment, I could see another figure in the distance, charging out

to welcome him home. I squeezed his hand and, with a heavy heart, kissed him goodbye.

He died two days later and when I heard the news, I wept as if I had lost my own father. We buried him, according to our custom, within forty-eight hours. The religious rituals seemed peculiarly unhelpful; the priests, as ever, spoke a lot about duty and honour and very little about grace and forgiveness. There was a curious, perfunctory nature about the way they conducted the service, as if they were anxious to end the era of embarrassment. I closed my eyes and thought of my dead master, I treasured the picture of him being welcomed home by his Father. 'He will meet you along the way...' Theodore's words will never leave me.

At the graveside, where the ground was hard as ice and the sky a perfect, crystal blue, representatives had gathered from the neighbouring families. As I watched them, it was clear that their fine words and solemn expressions betrayed no great sadness.

 This is the story of the prodigal son.

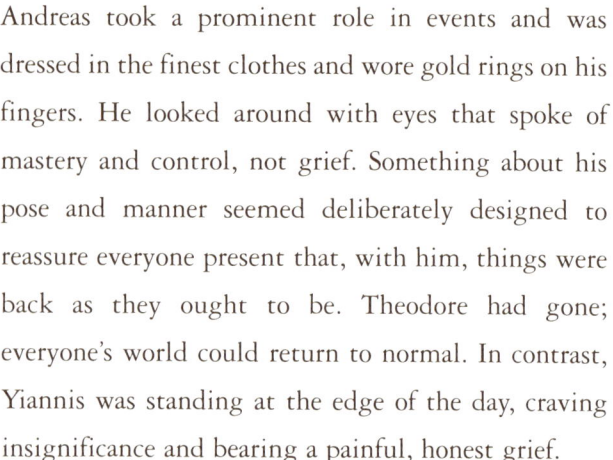

Andreas took a prominent role in events and was dressed in the finest clothes and wore gold rings on his fingers. He looked around with eyes that spoke of mastery and control, not grief. Something about his pose and manner seemed deliberately designed to reassure everyone present that, with him, things were back as they ought to be. Theodore had gone; everyone's world could return to normal. In contrast, Yiannis was standing at the edge of the day, craving insignificance and bearing a painful, honest grief.

And the common people? Well, they gathered around, keeping their respectful distance as was right and proper. Were they, I wondered, genuinely sad? I couldn't tell; I don't think they had ever really understood Theodore. Some of the wiser ones were, I thought, troubled, not so much by the loss of Theodore but at what – or who – was to come after him. Indeed, as I glanced at Andreas, tall, proud and taking stock with cold eyes, I felt a shiver of fear.

As soon as the first clods of earth were shovelled onto

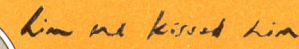 

the grave, I was not surprised to see Yiannis slipping away rapidly. He gave me a smile, raised a hand in a half salute of respect and left.

Two days later I was summoned into the presence of Andreas. Things had already changed at the house. There was now a guard at the door who demanded to know my business and whether I had an appointment. I ignored the insult, but when I had got past him I found myself before a clerk who consulted a list. Only then was I ushered into the presence of Lord Andreas. He had taken little time in establishing an office in his father's old study. The books, the worn carpet and the comfortable chairs had gone, and the old battered desk had been replaced by a shiny new one that seemed bigger and taller. Andreas sat behind it in a high-backed chair that might as well have been a throne.

I sat before him on a new, hard seat and he stared at me with calculating brown eyes. 'You served my father,' he said, and there was an unspoken question in his words.

'And, if it is your will, I will serve you,' I replied.

This is the story of the prodigal son.

'I joined the Salvadori Estate before you were born and the interests of your house have been mine ever since.'

He looked straight into my eyes; I think he was trying to intimidate me. 'Francis, know this. I am not my father. My father governed in a way that was lax. There will be changes.'

I gave a little bow of my head to acknowledge the truth of this but said nothing; I had decided to watch my words. Once upon a time, this might have been music to my ears. Now, I was not so sure.

He leaned back in his chair, watching me as a cat might watch a mouse. 'Three changes to start with. First, I want you to go over the accounts of the last twenty years and find every case in which my father was lenient. I want you to present me with those records a week from today. I am going to call in those debts.'

I nodded, fighting back the temptation to show my anger. 'It can be done,' I said slowly, battling the emotion in my voice.

... to him and hugged ... him and kissed him

'Second, I want all the tenancy agreements reviewed. My desire is to buy back the land that fool of a brother of mine lost. And to do that, I need to have the money. Put a 10 per cent surcharge on them all.'

He did not ask me what I thought. In fact, I knew he did not care what I thought. This was just as well, as I did not trust myself to answer him.

'And third, there is the issue of the common land. As you know, it has been a tradition that the people of the town may use it to graze their animals. But there is too much common land; some of it is too good to waste. Again, in a week's time, let me have a map of the common land and let us see what they don't need.'

Again, I simply nodded. 'Is there anything else, sir?'

'No, not for the moment. A week today. Remember.'

I stood to my feet. 'You may be assured, my Lord, that, as ever, my interest is the honour of your family.'

He didn't shake hands but sent me away with a dismissive gesture. Instead of returning to the office, I

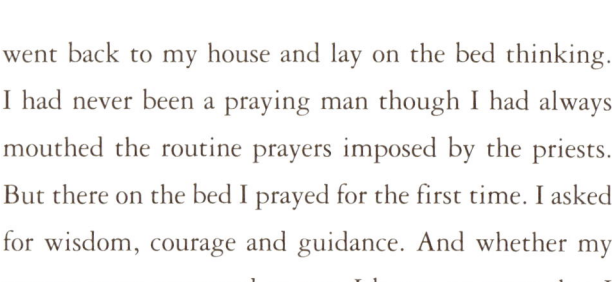

This is the story of the prodigal son.

went back to my house and lay on the bed thinking. I had never been a praying man though I had always mouthed the routine prayers imposed by the priests. But there on the bed I prayed for the first time. I asked for wisdom, courage and guidance. And whether my prayers were answered or not, I began to sense that I knew what I must do. Don't ask me how.

I arose, and headed back to the office as if it was business as usual. But there, I scribbled a single-lined note, sealed it and summoned a boy to deliver it. Then, with a heavy heart, I ordered that the first files of the last twenty years be delivered to my desk. That evening, after supper, I returned to my office and began to work through the oldest of them.

It was a bitter night, sprinkled with flurries of snow, and I knew there would be few people around. Just after eight, by my reckoning, the door creaked open and Despina's snow-kissed face appeared around it. She smiled. I locked the door behind her, pulled up two chairs by the fire and threw on another log.

ran to him and hugged him and kissed him

We sat facing each other, she slowly took her scarf and gloves off as a few last snowflakes melted into her hair.

'Thank you for coming, Despina,' I said.

'I presume you have your reasons.'

I nodded. 'Things are changing.'

'And not for the better.' Her face looked sad for a moment, but the melancholy gave way to a mischievous smile. 'But Francis, you can adapt, can't you? Doesn't the good steward adjust to the change of a master?'

I returned the smile.

'I talked with Andreas this morning. I–'

She raised a finger in interruption. 'Don't you mean, "My Lord Andreas"?'

'No, I do not. I was looking for a sign, Despina. Andreas obliged thrice over. He gave me three demands, all of which would have horrified his father. All of which horrify me.' I paused. 'And so, having spent over half

This is the story of the prodigal son.

my life here, it is time for me to leave.' I had no idea how Despina would react, but I braced myself.

'Where will you go?' she asked with an urgency that encouraged me.

'I have made no decision yet. The city, to begin with. Our late, beloved Lord Theodore gave me a wooden box in his will, full of gold crowns. There was also a small piece of paper on which he had written "You may need this".'

She nodded and I guessed that he had been similarly generous to her.

'I have to say, Despina, that I am adjusting my views of the Lord Theodore. I took him for granted while he lived but now he is gone and I have seen who has taken his place, I miss him more than I ever thought I would.'

Tears began to form in her eyes.

'I was thinking,' I said, 'about possibly buying a farm, a smallholding. Nothing much. I have been careful here and have saved some money. With that and my

Lord's gift, I can manage. I would need labour but I think it will work. So I will write my letter of resignation tomorrow and leave.'

'When?'

'Tomorrow evening. I will leave my resignation on my desk and slip away unnoticed.'

'I see.'

'I wanted to ask, do you have any plans?'

She stared at the fire. 'No, I do not think I will stay here long. Like you, I have already seen the signs. He struck one of the girls yesterday. Andreas seems to care little for all that his father held dear. In fact he seems to delight in trampling on it.'

There was one last part to my plan, and I suddenly became aware of my heart beating madly. Blood was rushing through my ears. Was I mad? I had truly changed. 'I was wondering if you would come with me?'

Mischief and longing crossed her features. 'Francis',

This is the story of  the prodigal son.

she paused, 'is that a business proposition or something more personal?'

'Actually…' I took a deep breath. 'It was meant as a proposal of marriage.'

'Are you so desperate that you are proposing to contaminate the fine family name of Nutrizio with my own?' She knew how to make me squirm.

'I have decided, rather belatedly, that there is more to life than honour,' I muttered. 'Despina…will you marry me?'

She paused for a moment – which felt like a lifetime. 'Francis, if you'd have asked me previously, I would have taken no time in politely declining your offer. I have found you heartless and cold.'

I bowed my head, trying to hide my embarrassment. 'A fair assessment of me indeed. May I ask you for forgiveness?'

'Granted, of course. But I'm fussy. I want a husband and a lover, not a steward.' I felt nervous and uneasy.

My usual composure abandoned me and I was humbled. 'But,' she added, 'I think you've changed.'

'Oh, I hope so,' I cried, honestly. 'I've done so much thinking recently about the brothers and their situation. I was critical – very critical – of Yiannis, and what he did was not right. Still, I have come to a conclusion. Every one of us is like him or Andreas. We are all, in our different ways, lost. But God has bought our forgiveness and restoration at an enormous cost. His unreserved and unlimited love is offered wholly and equally to both sons. We either accept that – as Yiannis did – or we reject it.'

'Ah, the penny has dropped!' There was wonderment and joy on her face.

'I'm a slow learner. But from what I can see, Andreas has rejected it. He might have stayed at home but he was lost all along. He refused to come home from a cold anger and self-pity that has made him such a stranger to his family. It seems that to reject this forgiveness is to choose a hard path...' I paused.

This is the story of the prodigal son.

'How slow I am, I didn't–'

'Yes.'

'Yes?'

'Yes, I *will* marry you. You have changed.'

I didn't realise how much I needed to hear Despina say those words until she did. It was a sort of homecoming in itself. Of course, looking back on this breathless night, I know now that I had grown to love her. But love, like life, is a strange creature. It's only when you look back along the road, sometimes, that you find you've taken that turn.

Despina gazed into the fire. Little needed to be said. She would come with me, she said. What was there to keep here here now?

'But which way do we go?'

For once, neither of us had an answer.

And so I returned to this very room, the backdrop to so many years, knowing that everything that had gone before had brought me to this point of no return. I was

leaving – we were leaving – and the road that stretched out ahead was unfamiliar, less travelled.

My letter of resignation did not take long to write. I packed those few things that I wanted to take with me. And then I began on this story: an exorcism, a baptism, a moment of sudden clarity that has taken so long, yet come so quickly.

Five short, blunt words. Beating at the door, ringing in my ears, shouting at the window on a dark, clear night; driving me to God-knows-where, to a place I might have glimpsed, but not yet seen; bereft of grid reference or signpost.

Which way do we go? Wherever it takes us, this road less travelled, this sacred path. One thing I now believe with all my heart: we're going home, however long it might take, whoever we might encounter. And me? I'm running as fast as my legs will carry me. It is time.

About the Author

J.John is a motivational speaker. His appeal transcends gender, age, culture and occupation. He helps people to see the spiritual dimension of life and he enables people to find a purpose to their everyday lives.